ORCA
Think

Question, connect and take action to become better citizens
with a brighter future. Now that's smart thinking!

REMEMBER THIS

The Fascinating World of Memory

Monique Polak

illustrated by Valéry Goulet

ORCA BOOK PUBLISHERS

Published in Canada and the United States in 2024 by Orca Book Publishers.
orcabook.com

Library and Archives Canada Cataloguing in Publication
Title: Remember this : the fascinating world of memory / Monique Polak ; illustrated by Valéry Goulet.
Names: Polak, Monique, author. | Goulet, Valéry, 1978- illustrator.
Series: Orca think ; 13.
Description: Series statement: Orca think ; 13 | Includes bibliographical references and index.
Identifiers: Canadiana (print) 20230197256 | Canadiana (ebook) 20230197264 |
ISBN 9781459834125 (hardcover) | ISBN 9781459834132 (PDF) | ISBN 9781459834149 (EPUB)
Subjects: LCSH: Memory—Juvenile literature.
Classification: LCC BF371 .P65 2024 | DDC j153.1/2—dc23

Library of Congress Control Number: 2023934391

Summary: This illustrated nonfiction book for middle-grade readers explores the art and
science of memory and what it can tell us about ourselves and the world we live in.

Orca Book Publishers is committed to reducing the consumption of nonrenewable resources in the
production of our books. We make every effort to use materials that support a sustainable future.

Orca Book Publishers gratefully acknowledges the support for its publishing programs provided
by the following agencies: the Government of Canada, the Canada Council for the Arts and the
Province of British Columbia through the BC Arts Council and the Book Publishing Tax Credit.

Cover and interior artwork by Valéry Goulet
Design by Dahlia Yuen
Edited by Kirstie Hudson

Printed and bound in South Korea.

27   26   25   24   •   1   2   3   4

In memory of my opa, Jo Spier (1900–1978),
who helped me write my first story and the smell of
whose cigars, all these years later, still makes me happy

Contents

INTRODUCTION

Close your eyes. What do you see?

Perhaps you're thinking back to something that happened this morning—how your dog jumped on your bed and licked your face, or how your brother hogged the bathroom when you needed to get in. Or maybe you're remembering something that happened in the more distant past—the fun you had on a family trip, or how sad you felt at your great-grandmother's funeral.

Memories are like houseguests. They turn up—sometimes uninvited. And like houseguests, some memories are fun to have around. Then there are others we can't wait to get rid of!

How does memory work? What is happening inside your brain when you are remembering? Why do we remember some things and forget others? Perhaps you and your best friend have entirely different memories of the day you met—why is that, and whose memory is right? Why does your grandfather forget the way back to the house he's lived in for 50 years? Are there tricks to help you memorize the math formulas for next week's test? Is there such a thing as photographic memory?

So many questions!

Most people associate memory with being grown-up or downright old. But kids have memories too. And as you will learn in this book, memories can be an important source of creative inspiration. All kinds of artists, including authors, filmmakers and even chefs, often get ideas from their memories.

Here's hoping that by reading this book you'll learn how memory works, tricks for improving memory (to help you on that math test) and perhaps even ways to use your own memories as a basis for a work of art—perhaps a story, video or meal!

1 HOW MEMORY WORKS

Let's say I ask you to remember your last birthday.

I bet a picture is forming in your mind. Perhaps you see yourself surrounded by friends and family, opening gifts. Do you hear your friends singing "Happy Birthday"? Can you almost taste your chocolate cake? Or maybe you are remembering the feeling of your grandfather holding you close as he hugs you, or the sulfury smell when you blow out the candles and make a wish.

Memories have a way of popping up in milliseconds. That's superquick, considering that a millisecond is one thousandth of a second!

> "God gave us memory so that we might have roses in December."
>
> —J.M. Barrie (1860–1937), Scottish novelist and creator of Peter Pan

WARNING!
WHAT COMES NEXT IS PRETTY TECHNICAL

What exactly is going on inside your brain when you remember? The answer is, *a lot*. And we don't understand all of it. Although scientists have spent years investigating how the human brain makes memories, they still have many unanswered questions. Here's what they've figured out so far.

Memory is the result of the activity of neural circuits in our brains. Now you must be wondering what neural circuits are. They're groups of neurons connected by synapses that carry out specific functions. Neurons send information to different parts of the brain using electrical impulses and chemical signals. As for synapses, they're pockets of space between two cells.

We also know there are three steps to remembering: ***encoding***, ***storing*** and ***retrieval***.

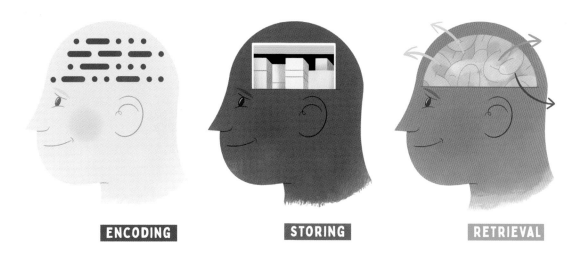

ENCODING **STORING** **RETRIEVAL**

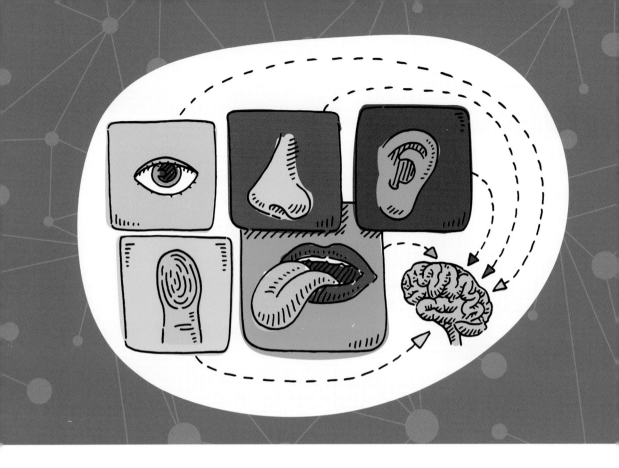

The brain takes in information from each of the five senses: sight, smell, hearing, touch and taste.

ENCODING

Encoding happens when we learn something or when information comes to us through the five senses. (That's why I mentioned *seeing* your birthday party, *hearing* your friends sing, *tasting* cake, *feeling* your grandfather's hug and *smelling* the sulfury smell as you blew out the candles.) Our senses allow us to perceive the world. Without them, we wouldn't have anything to remember.

A part of the brain called the **hippocampus** plays an important role in forming new memories. Located deep inside the brain, the hippocampus is shaped like a seahorse. Think of the hippocampus as a train station. Memories don't hang out there for long. Instead they get processed and sent off to be stored in the parts of the brain responsible for **long-term memory**.

If a person's hippocampus is damaged, it is more difficult to form new memories. We know, for example, that **Alzheimer's disease** affects the hippocampus. You have probably heard of Alzheimer's, a brain disorder that causes the brain to shrink and brain cells to die, leading to the deterioration of memory and thinking skills. Alzheimer's disease mostly affects older adults.

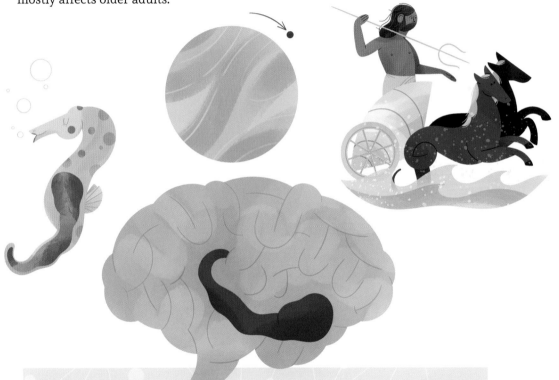

Hippo Who?

If you're like me, you like saying the word *hippocampus*. Maybe because it starts off like the word hippopotamus! It is believed that back in 1587, a Roman surgeon named Julius Caesar Arantius was the first to discover and describe this part of the brain. Noting its resemblance to a seahorse, Arantius called it the hippocampus. But he wasn't the one who came up with the word. In Greek and Roman mythology, the god of the sea, who is called Poseidon in Greek mythology and Neptune in the Roman, drives a chariot drawn by creatures called hippocampi. The top of these creatures' bodies looks like a horse, while the bottom is like a fish. In other words, they resemble seahorses. More recently, in 2019, a tiny moon orbiting the planet Neptune—about three billion miles from Earth—was named Hippocamp.

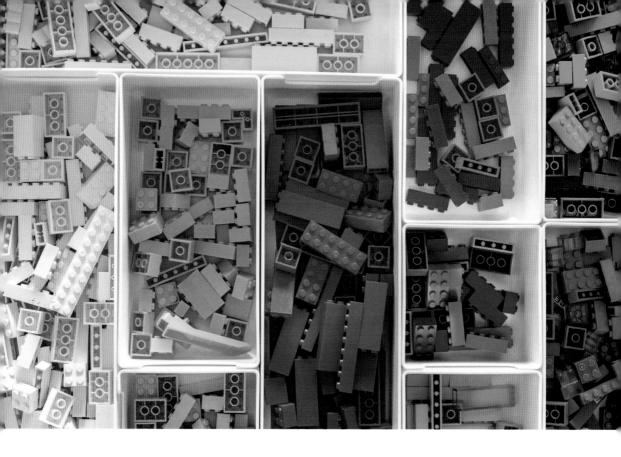

Like a well-organized box of LEGO, the brain stores information in a way that makes it easy to retrieve.

STORING

Storing is how we hold on to memories over time. The human brain is made up of about 100 billion neurons. Each neuron makes 1,000 or more connections to other neurons. So the human brain's memory storage is believed to be 2.5 petabytes—or a million gigabytes. That's about 4,000 times more memory than the 256 gigabytes of memory in my new laptop computer.

There are some memories we don't need to hold on to for very long. For example, let's say for a school project you are going to meet up at another kid's house. His address is 425 Green Avenue. "Will you remember that?" he asks. Of course! As you walk over to Green Avenue, you repeat the numbers 425 in your head. But if this is the last time you ever visit that house, you will not need to remember the address.

That's what **short-term memory** is for. Scientists have discovered that short-term memories are stored in a part of the brain called the **prefrontal cortex**.

Long-term memories are stored in many parts of the brain. According to scientists, only a few hours after the initial acquisition of a memory it is moved to long-term memory. What's amazing is that long-term memories get stored in so many different regions of the brain. Memories associated with each of the five senses, for example, are stored in five distinct areas. So when you are remembering something that happened long ago—like that birthday party—neural circuits are lighting up all over your brain.

RETRIEVAL

Retrieval is how we call up information when we need it. Another word for retrieval is *recall*. Quick! What was the name of your kindergarten teacher? What's the name of the book you read last summer? Sometimes the answers come immediately. Other times it's harder to access information. You are taking a test, for example, and you can't for the life of you remember the name of the first Indigenous woman to launch into space. (By the way, it was Nicole Aunapu Mann, a member of the Round Valley Indian Tribes.)

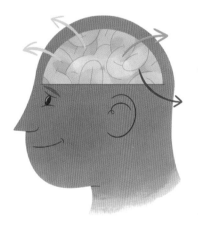

Delicious Memories

Many professional chefs find inspiration in their earliest food memories. Cara Chigazola-Tobin, the chef-owner at Honey Road in Burlington, Vermont, still remembers the elaborate meals her grandmother prepared, especially for holidays. "She would set me up at the kitchen table with a basket of beans and a bowl full of pickles. I would eat pickles, watch her daytime soap operas and shuck black-eyed peas…Those dinners…hooked me into the food industry," Chigazola-Tobin said in an interview with the Vermont Fresh Network.

SOME WORDS WORTH REMEMBERING

You've already learned some important terms having to do with memory—such as *neurons*, *hippocampus*, *short-* and *long-term memory*. It's time for me to introduce you to a few more. Ready?

Amnesia refers to memory loss that is usually temporary. Amnesia can be caused by head or brain injury, traumatic events, alcohol or certain drugs.

Episodic memory is memory of a past event or episode, such as that birthday party I asked you to remember. These memories are autobiographical—meaning we can use them to tell the story of our lives.

Flashbulb memory is memory associated with learning about a major, usually disturbing public event. Ask your parents where they were on September 11, 2001, when they learned that New York City's Twin Towers had been destroyed by terrorists, and they will almost certainly be able to tell you.

> *"I am a bear of very little brain, and long words bother me."*
> —Pooh Bear in *Winnie-the-Pooh* by A.A. Milne (1882–1956), English writer

Poppins Popularizes Superlong Word

Probably because they have many syllables, long words are harder to remember than shorter ones. My favorite long word—*supercalifragilisticexpialidocious*—was made famous by the 1964 movie *Mary Poppins*. Mary, played by actress Julie Andrews, sings a song called—you guessed it!—"Supercalifragilisticexpialidocious." Pretty much every kid who saw that movie and heard the song managed to learn this 34-letter word. That's because, as you will read later in this book, it's easier to remember something if you put it to music, if it's funny or if you have a happy association with it.

Longest Words in the English Language

At 45 letters long, the word *pneumonoultramicroscopicsilicovolcanoconiosis* is the longest word in the English language. It is an invented word that refers to a condition caused by the inhalation of fine silicate or quartz dust. The word *hippopotomonstrosesquippedaliophobia* is less long, having 36 letters. Ironically, it refers to the fear of long words!

Memory triggers are any kind of stimuli that cause us to recall memories. For instance, every time you smell tomato sauce you instantly remember your babysitter, who makes the world's best tomato sauce.

Procedural memory is long-term memory for knowing how to do stuff such as walk or play piano. These are also known as motor skills.

Mnemonics are techniques to improve memory. Mnemonics are believed to have been invented by the ancient Greeks. The word *mnemonics* comes from Mnemosyne, the Greek goddess of memory.

Semantic memory is long-term memory for information that is not connected to particular events or contexts. An example of semantic memory is being able to remember the names of Canada's last three prime ministers or of the last three US presidents.

Muscle memory allows us to remember a particular movement without having to think about it. That's because we've repeated and practised the muscular movement so many times. Some examples are riding a bicycle or entering your password on your computer. Though I skied a lot when I was a kid, I stopped for nearly 40 years. When I got off the chairlift after so many years, my knees wobbled. But I needn't have worried. My muscle memory kicked in, and soon I was zipping down the hill!

MEET BRENDA MILNER, MEMORY EXPERT

2

Brenda Milner has received honorary degrees from more than 25 universities around the world.

Some of the most important discoveries about how memory works have been made by a neuroscientist named Brenda Milner. Born in Manchester, England, in 1918, Milner moved to Montreal in 1944. Milner was the first neuroscientist to discover where in the brain memories are formed. This discovery was based on her work with a patient named Henry Molaison, who is called H.M. in the many scientific papers written about him. Before Milner met him, H.M. had suffered from severe epileptic seizures. To stop his seizures, doctors removed a part of his brain. Though the seizures ended, the surgery left H.M. incapable of forming new memories. Milner concluded that it was the loss of H.M.'s hippocampus that prevented him from forming new memories. She was the first neuroscientist to understand the critical role of the hippocampus.

CURIOSITY RULES

Milner believes in the power of curiosity and observation. After all, it was curiosity and observation that led to her discovery. "It was a big surprise," Milner told me in a phone interview, "when I was working with H.M., who was not remembering anything from moment to moment but who had perfectly normal learning of a motor skill such as drawing from a mirror image." For most people, tracing a figure on paper by seeing only a mirror image of the drawing is difficult at first. But with practice, they get the hang of it. Which is what happened with H.M.

Though the surgery H.M. underwent left him with permanent amnesia, or unable to form new memories, his motor learning was not affected. "Motor learning is basic, for example, to all sports," Milner explained.

Henry Molaison, called H.M. in scientific papers, is considered the most famous patient in the history of neuroscience.
JENNI OGDEN, JENNIOGDEN.COM

MEMORY EXPERT'S EARLIEST MEMORIES

I asked Milner about her own earliest memories. "I remember back to when I was around two, living in Manchester. I remember my father very much," she told me. Milner's father was the music critic for the *Guardian* newspaper. "Dad was always at home in the mornings. I remember that he grew delphiniums and was very interested in colors. I remember going with my dad to buy fabric for a dress for my mother," said Milner.

Milner also remembers how, when she was a little girl, her father read Shakespeare's plays to her. "In high school I told my classmates that I knew all of Shakespeare's work," she recalled, chuckling at the memory. Milner went to the University of Cambridge to study math. But she soon realized she was more interested in psychology than math.

> *"Remember tonight... for it is the beginning of always."*
> —Dante Alighieri (1265–1321), Italian poet

Not Everyone Gets a School Named After Them

In 2019 Brenda Milner attended the opening ceremony for the Ecole régionale Brenda-Milner (ERBM). Located in Châteauguay, Quebec, the school has 97 students, all of whom have intellectual disabilities and many of whom also have motor difficulties or are on the autism spectrum. "Everything about this school is special," said Manon Couturier, a resource teacher at ERBM. Facilities include a therapeutic pool, music-therapy room and multisensory rooms. "Multisensory rooms help calm our students down," explained Couturier. Most students at ERBM are nonverbal. There is a preschool class, as well as primary and secondary classes. Couturier says she will not forget meeting Brenda Milner at the ceremony. "She inspired me. She seemed curious and interested in everything around her," said Couturier.

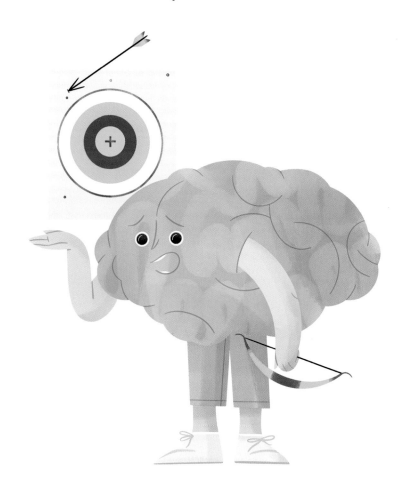

YOU CAN'T TRUST IT!

One of Milner's professors, Frederic Bartlett, was an important influence on her scientific career. Bartlett, the author of a book called *Remembering: A Study in Experimental and Social Psychology*, was famous for his work on the unreliability of memory. "We all studied that book," said Milner.

It was from Bartlett that Milner learned one of the most important lessons about memory—not to trust it! "Warn your readers that memory is unreliable. Memories become changed with repetition. The degree of confidence you have about a memory is not related to the accuracy," Milner explained.

Bartlett's Memory Experiments

Psychologist Frederic Bartlett wanted to understand what happens to memory over time. His most famous experiments in this area involved what Bartlett claimed was an Indigenous folktale called "The War of the Ghosts." (Interestingly, there is no evidence the tale originated with Indigenous Peoples. In fact, it was common in Bartlett's time for white people to attribute folktales to Indigenous Peoples.) In one experiment, Bartlett read the tale in question out loud twice to participants and 15 minutes later asked them to recall what he had read. He continued testing participants' memory of the tale over time. Some were even asked to remember the tale 10 years later. Not surprisingly, participants remembered less as time passed. They also interpreted the tale in different ways.

In a second experiment, which may remind you of the party game Broken Telephone, Bartlett told the tale to one person, who, after a set period of time, retold the tale to someone else, who in turn told someone else and so on. Bartlett wrote down the retellings and observed that the tale changed a lot. Participants changed it in ways that would help them make better sense of it. For example, many of them changed "hunting seals" to "fishing" since they had never hunted seals.

Bartlett concluded that memory is **constructive**—meaning we help create it. According to Bartlett, we build memories by connecting them to our past reactions and experiences. He also noted that many memories are linked to "a little outstanding detail which commonly appears in image or in language form."

OBJECTS THAT HELP US REMEMBER

3

The French word for a memory is *un souvenir*. The French verb *se souvenir* means "to remember." In English, the word **souvenir** refers to an object that serves as a memento to help us remember a place, experience or person—and sometimes all three.

A WAY TO REMEMBER HAPPY TIMES

We have many souvenir shops in Montreal. Tourists visit these shops to buy presents for family and friends but also to remind themselves of the fun they had here. They may choose caps or coffee mugs that say *Montreal* or snow globes of the city skyline. It's because people enjoy remembering happy times, such as being on holiday, that souvenir shops stay in business.

When I was 12, my family and I visited Mount Vesuvius, an active volcano in southern Italy. In 79 CE the volcano erupted, burying the city of Pompeii in black lava. I don't remember much about Vesuvius except peering into a giant hole. But I do remember that my dad bought my sister and me each a bracelet made from black lava. Though I don't know what became of that bracelet, I can still picture it—three rows of shiny bluish black stones strung together with elastic—and feel the way it clung (a little too snugly) on my wrist.

Meaningful objects help us remember and preserve or hold on to the past.

> "We are all the pieces of what we remember. We hold in ourselves the hopes and fears of those who love us.
>
> As long as there is love and memory, there is no true loss."
>
> —Cassandra Clare (1973–), American author (her real name is Judith Lewis)

Top-Selling Souvenirs

In 2021 the French travel company Club Med came out with a list of top-selling souvenirs, arranged by country. Here are a few items from that list. If you ever visit any of these places, keep some room in your luggage.

Canada: maple syrup
Egypt: papyrus scroll
Jamaica: Blue Mountain coffee
Japan: origami paper

Korea: tea
Poland: amber jewelry
Tunisia: ceramic plate
Uganda: banana-fiber toy

OBJECTS THAT HELP US GET THROUGH HARD TIMES

Some objects take on a special significance for us because they were there when we moved from one stage of life to another or when we experienced difficulties. Psychologists call these **transitional objects**. Because they are frequently used by kids, transitional objects are often fuzzy or cuddly—like a teddy bear or favorite blanket. "Transitional objects help you make sense of the world and get through a difficult time," said Jon Fein, a documentary filmmaker whom you will read about later in this chapter.

Open up Geneviève Alexander's closet and you'll find a brown teddy bear on the floor. "I would never throw him out," she told me. Alexander, who was one of my students at Marianopolis College and was 17 when I spoke with her for this book, was adopted when she was six months old. "When my parents went to pick me up at the foster house, I was waiting in a car seat, and the bear was next to me," she explained. The bear was twice the size of baby Geneviève. Alexander believes the bear will always be important to her. "It makes me remember that I was once really, really tiny, that I used to be a vulnerable child, but now I've grown into an independent woman still trying to figure out who she is," she said.

Geneviève Alexander's teddy bear helped her navigate a difficult time as a child.
GENEVIÈVE ALEXANDER

MY MOM'S CHILDHOOD DRESS

My mother, Celein, kept a transitional object for most of her life. It was an embroidered silk dress she wore when she was three years old. My mother was 13 and living in the Netherlands when, in 1943, she and her family were rounded up by the Nazis and transported to Theresienstadt, a concentration camp in what is now the Czech Republic.

She was allowed to bring only one small suitcase. In addition to packing necessities, my mother tucked that dress into her suitcase.

During the nearly two years my mother was imprisoned at Theresienstadt, this transitional object served to remind her of her life before the Holocaust. When Theresienstadt was liberated in 1945 and my mother and her family returned to the Netherlands, the dress came back with her. She kept it for more than 60 years, eventually giving it to me. Today the dress hangs in my closet, reminding me every time I open the closet door about my mother and her story. One day, when I am ready, I will bring my mother's dress to the Montreal Holocaust Museum, where others will be able to see it too and learn my mother's story.

JULIE MAYFENG/SHUTTERSTOCK.COM

MUSEUMS HELP US REMEMBER

Museums store and exhibit objects. In this way they help us preserve societal memories—historical memories shared by members of a community.

One powerful example of a museum working to preserve societal memories is the Museum of Memory and Human Rights. Located in Santiago, Chile, this museum, which opened in 2010, is dedicated to the victims of human rights violations during the military dictatorship of Augusto Pinochet between 1973 and 1990. Thousands of Chileans were tortured and murdered during Pinochet's rule.

The museum's exhibits include legal documents, letters, photos of victims and video coverage of protests that took place while Pinochet was in power. Also on exhibit are arpilleras, Spanish for "burlap." These are handmade patchwork pictures, most produced by women during Pinochet's dictatorship. The arpilleras serve as powerful reminders of history. They also remind us of the need to protect human rights and work hard to avoid repeating the terrible mistakes of the past.

Chile's Museum of Memory and Human Rights opened 20 years after Pinochet was deposed, or forced from office. That is sooner than usual. "Museums have traditionally only kept things that have been at least 50 years old," documentary filmmaker Jon Fein told me.

This display from Chile's Museum of Memory and Human Rights shows photographs of people who went missing or were murdered during the military dictatorship of Augusto Pinochet.

YASEMIN OLGUNOZ BERBER/
SHUTTERSTOCK.COM

The bright blue lights in the 9/11 memorial *Tribute in Light* remind us where the World Trade Center's Twin Towers once stood.

REMEMBERING THE TRAGEDY OF 9/11

On the morning of September 11, 2001, Fein was on a train to New York City to meet his filmmaking partner, Brian Danitz. "When we got to the northernmost station, we could see the smoke from the Twin Towers," Fein recalled. He and his fellow passengers were not allowed to disembark in Manhattan. On the day of the attack, people were already collecting artifacts and objects. This gave Fein and Danitz the idea for their next film. "People were preserving history while it happened, [and] we realized this was an important story to capture. It seemed like that in itself was history we should be preserving," said Fein.

The pair spent seven years collecting objects, including a pair of bloodied shoes, an ID card and a police badge, as well as stories for their film *Objects and Memory*, a made-for-TV documentary about how people attempt to preserve their memories of traumatic events such as 9/11, the Oklahoma City bombing and the Vietnam War.

Fein is fascinated by the connection between objects and stories. "Without a story, an object is meaningless.

But without an object, our stories are less vibrant. One of my objectives is to remind people that otherwise ordinary things mean the most because of their associations with people, places and events," Fein said. He also believes that in some way, objects carry the essence of the people to whom they were important. This helps explain why Fein and his wife are unable to throw out several outdated engineering books that once belonged to Fein's father-in-law.

A PAIR OF TWO-DOLLAR BILLS TELLS A REMARKABLE STORY

One story in *Objects and Memory* involves a two-dollar bill that a woman named Myrta Gschaar shared with the film-makers. Gschaar's husband, Robert, died in the Twin Towers. "Myrta told us that when Robert proposed in 1988, it would be a second marriage for both of them. He pulled out two two-dollar bills from his wallet and told Myrta, 'They represent us.' He showed her that if you flipped over the two twos, the mirror image is a heart. Both kept their two-dollar bills in their wallets," said Fein. Several months after 9/11, New York City police recovered Robert's wallet.

Myrta donated Robert's two-dollar bill to New York City's 9/11 Memorial and Museum. She also gave the museum the two-dollar bill she had kept in her own wallet. When museum visitors see those two-dollar bills and learn the Gschaars' story, they gain a deeper, more personal understanding of the losses associated with 9/11. Fein believes that the most successful memorial museums have a mission. "I always say that for me, it's not about 9/11; it's about 9/12, which is when people asked themselves, 'What can I do to help?'" said Fein.

4 FLASHBULB MEMORIES

You've seen what happens when you take a photo and use the flash. There's a burst of light, and for a moment everything looks brighter. The same happens with flashbulb memories.

SHARP AND BRIGHT

As you learned in chapter 1, a flashbulb memory is a memory of learning about something major, often shocking. It is not a memory of the event itself—it's a memory of learning *about* the event. Flashbulb memories feel sharp and bright.

The term was introduced in 1977 by psychologists Roger Brown and James Kulik. The pair studied people's memories of the 1963 assassination of US president John F. Kennedy. They found that flashbulb memories are usually clear and long-lasting.

Not all flashbulb memories have to do with something terrible. Some are connected to positive events. For example,

"Different people remember things differently, and you'll not get any two people to remember anything the same, whether they were there or not."

—Neil Gaiman (1960–), English writer, from *The Ocean at the End of the Lane*

the fall of the Berlin Wall on November 9, 1989, marked the end of what was called the Cold War. The wall, which separated East and West Berlin, dated back to 1961 and was a long-time symbol of a divided Germany.

Most flashbulb memories, however, are connected to learning about disturbing or shocking events, such as Kennedy's assassination or the 2004 earthquake and tsunami in Indonesia.

WHERE WERE YOU?

Most people who were alive in 1997 probably remember learning of the death of Princess Diana. The same is true for those who were alive on September 11, 2001, a day you read about in chapter 3. Most of us who were alive on 9/11 can remember where we were when we learned of the shocking event, what we were doing, who broke the news and how we felt.

A Rosebush by the Door

American psychologist Frederick Welton Colgrove was one of the first researchers to observe flashbulb memory in action, even though he did not use the term. Colgrove reported on a study that took place 33 years after the 1865 assassination of Abraham Lincoln, the 16th president of the United States. One hundred and seventy-nine participants were asked to share their recollection of the moment when they learned of Lincoln's murder, which took place at Ford's Theatre in Washington, DC. Colgrove was struck by the level of detail in the participants' recollections. One participant, a 79-year-old woman, recalled, "I was setting out a rosebush by the door. My husband came in the yard and told me."

Mourners set up this impromptu memorial outside Kensington Palace following the tragic death of Princess Diana.
ALBERT A T/FLICKR.COM

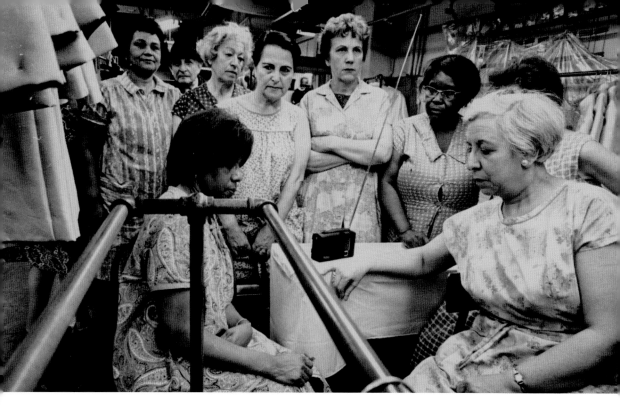

REMEMBERING EVENTS THAT MATTER TO US

Brown and Kulik believe it is precisely a person's emotional reaction at the time that makes a flashbulb memory so strong. The pair also identified another factor that influences the development of flashbulb memories: ***relevance***. They found that if an event is personally meaningful or relevant to us, we are more likely to have a clear memory of learning about it.

Brown and Kulik found, for example, that 75 percent of Black people had a vivid memory of learning about the April 4, 1968, assassination of Martin Luther King, Jr., leader of the American Civil Rights Movement. King led the 1955 Montgomery bus boycott in which Black citizens in Montgomery, Alabama, protested their bus system's policy of racial segregation. Brown and Kulik found, however, that only 33 percent of white Americans alive at the time had a vivid memory of learning about King's assassination.

LEARNING OF A TRAGIC EXPLOSION

On August 4, 2020, ammonium nitrate stored at the Port of Beirut in Lebanon exploded. More than 200 people were killed, and an estimated 7,000 were injured in the explosion. At the time Kyra Simatos was 15 years old and a student at Collège Stanislas de Montréal. The Beirut explosion was personally meaningful and relevant to her. Her mother was born in Lebanon, and Simatos had spent many summers there when she was growing up. She had friends and family in Beirut, including her aunt, whose apartment was near the port, as well as an uncle, whose newborn son, Zayn, Simatos had not yet met.

Simatos remembers exactly where she was and how she felt when she learned of the tragedy. "I was at the Yorkdale Mall in Toronto with my friends. I was sitting on a bench next to Restoration Hardware, and I kept hearing the words *Beirut* and *explosion*. I looked at Instagram, and all my friends and family in Beirut were posting. I started shaking and bawling my eyes out," Simatos told me.

She remembers crying as she messaged about 100 people. "I had friends whose arms were full of glass shards. Luckily, many kids in Lebanon do Scouts and are trained in first aid," she recalled.

Breaking News

In a column he wrote for the *Montreal Gazette* in 2021, journalist Mike Boone shared his flashbulb memory of learning about John F. Kennedy's assassination. The date was November 22, 1963, and Boone was a tenth-grade student in Montreal. Here's how Boone remembers the day: "Afternoon history class was disrupted when the teacher was summoned to the office. The all-boys class had no clue what was happening. None of us had smartphones—or any phones at all—in 1963." The boys' teacher—Boone remembers that his name was Walter Herring and that he had a second job as a news editor for a local television station—returned to the classroom and "in his sombre TV voice, Herring told us Kennedy had been shot." After that, Boone writes, "my memory gets a bit hazy." For Boone the flashbulb memory occurred at the moment his teacher broke the news of the attempt on the president's life. Kennedy's death was confirmed later that day.

MEMORIES THAT STICK

Flashbulb memories formed during adolescence and early adulthood—such as Simatos's—are extra strong and long-lasting. In 2010 researchers Jenny Denver, Swan Lane and Katie Cherry found that older adults were better able to retain flashbulb memories formed when they were adolescents or young adults than from more recent events.

But new research demonstrates that flashbulb memories are less accurate than we think they are. Although flashbulb memories feel superclear, they are actually subject to misremembering. Memories are subject to change. In fact, researchers have found that every single time we recall a memory, we alter it. Which means that with time and every retelling, memories—even the ones that feel supersharp—become less accurate.

Because memories have been shown to become less accurate over time, photographs can help us remember the details of our pasts.
JENA ARDELL/GETTY IMAGES

THERE'S SOMETHING ABOUT THAT SMELL!

5

I don't know the name of the cigars my grandfather used to smoke. But nearly 50 years after his death, I still recognize their smell. It's happened more than once that I've been walking in downtown Montreal and I get a whiff of something delicious. Someone up ahead is smoking the brand of cigar my grandfather favored—and I keep walking just to enjoy the odor. Of course, it isn't really about the odor. It's about the memories the familiar old smell evokes. While I sniff that cigar smoke, I remember my grandfather—the person to whom I felt closest when I was a kid.

> *"The true art of memory is the art of attention."*
>
> —Samuel Johnson
> (1709–1784), English writer

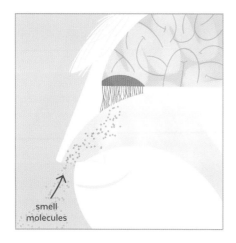

smell molecules

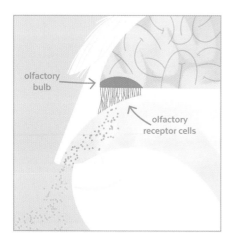

olfactory bulb

olfactory receptor cells

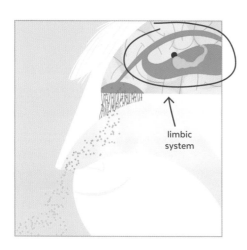

limbic system

SNIFFING AROUND INSIDE THE BRAIN

Smells do have a way of triggering memories. But why is that? Smell is our oldest sense. When we are born, smell is the first of our five senses to be activated. Some studies suggest that we can detect smells when we are still in our mothers' wombs.

Neuroscientists have been studying the connection between smell and memory. Smells are molecules from volatile substances—gases or chemicals that evaporate at room temperature to form a vapor—drifting in the air. When these molecules drift our way, neurons that make up our olfactory receptor cells send a signal to a part of the brain called the **olfactory bulb**. The olfactory bulb runs from the nose to the front of the brain. The olfactory bulb then sends information to other areas of the brain. Smells take a direct route to what is called the **limbic system**, which includes the **amygdala** and the hippocampus. The amygdala is connected to emotion; the hippocampus, to memory.

Smell is a more powerful trigger of memory than any of our other senses. That's because the brain's receptors for sight, taste, touch and sound all pass through a part of the brain called the **thalamus**, whose job it is to relay information to the **cerebral cortex**. Smell bypasses the thalamus. Typically a smell triggers an emotion before an actual memory. So when I smell that cigar smoke, I feel happy and loved. But if I came across a drawing or photo of one of my grandfather's cigars, I would be more likely to remember my grandfather's face (or his bald head!).

OUR NOSES HELP US SURVIVE

Neuroscientists think there is a reason why smell is so important, and the reason is connected to evolution. The sense of smell has contributed to our survival. Even simple single-celled organisms can detect smell. There is evidence that single-celled organisms use their sense of smell to interact with chemicals around them. Scientists who studied colonies of soil bacteria found that these bacteria could detect the smell of airborne ammonia, needed for bacteria to grow.

There's more. For many animals, the sense of smell is essential for survival. Organisms with smell receptors can sniff out food, possible danger and even mating partners! Elephants rely on their sense of smell to locate and remember watering and feeding spots. Our sense of smell helps us humans survive too. Have you ever smelled rotten fish? Way too stinky to eat, right? So that putrid odor may protect us from possible food poisoning.

An elephant smells by using its long trunk, which is a combination of nose and upper lip. The African elephant has more smell receptors than any other mammal, including dogs.
ODD HACKWELDER/SHUTTERSTOCK.COM

Look After Your Nose

Neuroscientist Rachel Herz believes keeping our sense of smell healthy is vital for mental and physical health. Here are some Dos and Don'ts to keep your sniffer sniffing at full capacity.

- *Do* stay away from chemicals—such as the ones in cleaning products—that emit strong fumes.
- *Do* wear a mask if you are exposed to fumes for a long time, even from everyday items such as cleaning or nail-polish products.
- *Do* protect your head and sinuses. Head injuries and sinus infections can cause a decline in our sensitivity to smell.
- *Do* exercise your nose. In case you're wondering how that works, here's Herz's advice: "Pay attention to smells. Deliberately sniff lots of different things every day."
- *Don't* smoke!

These two are enjoying the fragrance of sweet peas, which smell like orange blossom, hyacinth and rose.

SKUNKS AND ASPHALT

Neuroscientist Rachel Herz studies the connection between smell and memory. A professor at the Warren Elpert Medical School of Brown University in Providence, Rhode Island, Herz is the author of *The Scent of Desire: Discovering Our Enigmatic Sense of Smell*.

You may have wondered why you love the smell of popcorn while the same smell makes your best friend nauseous. Herz believes there is no such thing as a good or bad smell. "Liking or disliking a smell is based on personal or cultural learning," she told me. In particular, Herz explained, we are affected by what are called "first exposures"—our first encounters with a particular smell. Here is an example from Herz's life. Unlike most people, Herz likes the smell of skunk. "My earliest smell memory was when I was four, riding in the back seat of my parents' car in the countryside around Ithaca, New York. The windows were rolled down, and I remember my mom saying, 'Oh, I love that smell.' It turned out to be the smell of skunk. I'd never smelled it before, but it became coded with positive meaning because of the positive experience I was having," Herz said.

For Herz, the smell of skunk evokes a specific auto-biographical memory—that moment in the back seat of her parents' car. Herz has another smell-evoked autobiographical memory that also takes her back to her parents' car, only this memory is less pleasant. Herz was in the back seat again, this time feeling carsick on a drive from Montreal to New York. "They were asphalting the road, and I felt like throwing up. I still hate the smell of creosote or tar," she said.

ODORS AND ILLNESS

There was a lot of talk about smell during the COVID-19 pandemic, which struck our planet in March 2020. That's because 85 percent of people with mild cases of the virus lost their sense of smell. For 95 percent of those people, the loss was temporary, and they regained their sense of smell within six months. Which leaves the other 5 percent contending with a long-lasting loss of smell.

As we grow older, especially after middle age, our sense of smell fades.

The loss of smell has also been linked to depression. People who suffer from depression often have reduced olfactory performance—meaning they don't perceive the presence of scents as well as they used to. "Sensitivity to smell declines in people who are depressed. And the loss of the sense of smell can lead to depression," said Herz.

Herz believes we need to pay more attention to smell and the memories it evokes. "Most people don't give their sense of smell the importance it deserves. Memories make up the stories of our lives. The memories connected to smell are the most emotional and bring us back most vividly to those past times and places," she said.

Elephants Never Forget

There's truth to the old expression "elephants never forget." Besides being able to remember watering and feeding spots and migration routes, elephants remember other elephants—and people! Elephants' strong sense of smell has a lot to do with their having an excellent memory. If you observe elephants, you will notice how they move their trunks back and forth—that's how they detect scents. Elephants have more scent receptors and larger olfactory bulbs than any other mammal. In one study, elephants were shown to be able to distinguish the urine scents of as many as 30 female relatives—even those from whom they had been separated for years.

In 1999 two elephants had an emotional reunion at the Elephant Sanctuary in Hohenwald, Tennessee. Jenny, one of the sanctuary's resident elephants, became agitated when a new elephant named Shirley turned up. Staff members were surprised when both elephants started bellowing. It turned out that 23 years earlier, Jenny and Shirley had been part of the same traveling circus!

WORKING MEMORY

6

"Can you feed the dog after school?"

"Don't forget to have a parent sign the permission slip so you can come on next week's class trip."

"Open your science textbook to page 63. We'll start by looking at the second graph at the bottom of the page."

Feeding the dog, getting that permission slip signed and finding the second graph at the bottom of page 63 are all tasks that require **working memory**.

As creatures of habit, dogs appreciate a regular feeding routine.
DRAGON IMAGES/SHUTTERSTOCK.COM

33

STICKY NOTES INSIDE THE BRAIN

Working memory lets us hold on to information temporarily. Think of it as sticky notes for the brain. Researchers believe working memory begins to develop when we are between six and eight months old. It continues to develop as children acquire language and attention skills. Working memory makes learning possible. It is considered one of the brain's *executive functions*, meaning it helps us plan ahead and achieve our goals.

As we age, our working memory declines. Maybe that's why so many of us adults rely on to-do lists! But there are also many kids who have trouble making memory.

"Did you mention something about the dog?"

"Shoot! I left the permission slip at home!"

"What page are we supposed to open to?"

Kids with learning differences, such as *attention-deficit/ hyperactivity disorder (ADHD)* and executive-functioning issues, often have poor working memory. They may find it difficult to follow instructions and may appear to be inattentive or easily distracted. Luckily, there are solutions.

> *"Children use the fist until they are of age to use the brain."*
>
> —Elizabeth Barrett Browning (1806-1861), English poet who began writing poetry at age 11

Mattresses, Pillows and Memory

What do mattresses and pillows have to do with memory? Well, some are filled with what's called memory foam—a soft, cushiony material that over time "remembers" your body shape and favorite sleeping position. Memory foam was invented in 1966 at a National Aeronautics and Space Administration (NASA) facility called Ames Research Center. NASA wanted to keep pilots comfortable and safer during test flights. Today memory foam is also used in football helmets and motorcycle seats. In 2005 a company named Equine Prosthetics used memory foam to design a prosthesis for Thor, a thoroughbred horse whose injuries had left him with a nonfunctioning hind foot. Had it not been for the prosthesis, Thor would have been put down. Instead he went on to do hospital visits with children who were facing amputation and prosthetic replacement of their limbs.

TRICKS TO BOOST YOUR WORKING MEMORY

MAKE A LIST.

Take a lesson from us older folks. I never go to the grocery store without my shopping list, because if I did, I know I'd forget something! So if you have a list of, say, stuff to do for homework, write it down. The simple act of writing helps your working memory. Having a list also helps reduce the stress associated with having to remember stuff. An added benefit is that crossing items off the list (for instance, once an assignment is completed) feels *amazing*!

CHUNK IT UP.

Break information into chunks so it's easier to remember. Rather than remembering the 100 or so items on your bucket list, chunk items into groups. What places do you hope to visit? Who do you hope to meet? What good things do you want to contribute to the world? Chunks are easier to remember than individual items.

SAY IT OVER AGAIN AND OUT LOUD.

Simple repetition works. Repeating what you've heard helps you remember it. Saying it out loud so you hear the words you want to remember provides an added boost to working memory.

GET MUSICAL.

Turn what you want to remember into a poem or song—then sing it. Because this technique is fun, it helps reduce stress. Try it, and you'll see it works!

Writing out multiplication tables and then reading them over and over is a good way to memorize them.

CAROL YEPES/GETTY IMAGES

USE MNEMONICS.

The word *mnemonics* is hard to pronounce (nuh-mah-niks) and spell. It refers to a technique that helps us remember certain facts by using an acronym, rhyme, sentence or other tool. I still remember being 10 years old and reading that if I wanted to remember the colors of the spectrum, all I had to do was remember the name Roy G. Biv. The *R* in Roy stands for red, the *o* for orange, the *y* for yellow, the *G* in between for green, the *B* in Biv for blue, the *I* for indigo and the *v* for violet. All these years later, I still remember the Roy G. Biv trick, proving that mnemonics work!

PACIFIC   MOUNTAIN   CEN...   EASTERN   ATLANTIC   NEWFOUNDLAND & LABRADOR

PRIME MINISTER

Because I Know You Want More Mnemonics!

My very excellent mother just served us nine pizzas. This mnemonic will help you remember the order of the planets from the sun: Mercury, Venus, Earth, Mars, Jupiter, Saturn, Uranus, Neptune and—though it is no longer considered a planet—Pluto. Or you can try learning it this way:

My very excellent mother just served us nachos. Same planets but without Pluto.

Please excuse my dear Aunt Sally will help you during a math test when you're trying to remember the order of operations to work out equations: parentheses, exponents, multiply, divide, add, subtract.

Prime ministers can't eat any nachos— more nachos? This mnemonic is for Canadians wanting to remember our country's time zones: Pacific, Mountain, Central, Eastern, Atlantic, Newfoundland and Labrador.

Super Man helps every one. Use this mnemonic to learn the order of the Great Lakes from west to east: Superior, Michigan, Huron, Erie, Ontario.

MEMORIZE THIS!

7

At one time or another, you will need to memorize something for school. Maybe it's the names of the world's 10 highest mountains or Canada's 13 capital cities.

WHAT'S THE POINT OF MEMORIZING STUFF?

Does memorization work? You may be able to list the world's 10 highest mountains or Canada's capital cities on next week's quiz, but will you remember those names 10 or even 50 years from now? The answer is, it depends. Research indicates that if we continue to draw on material we have memorized, that material will move to our long-term memory. If you never think of those mountains again after next week's quiz, all the work you did memorizing their names will probably be lost.

> *"If you wish to forget anything on the spot, make a note that this thing is to be remembered."*
>
> —Edgar Allan Poe (1809–1849), American writer

When I was little and my mom needed a break, she'd send me to my room to memorize a poem. I can still rattle off dozens of poems from Robert Louis Stevenson's collection *A Child's Garden of Verses*. But over the years I've continued to practice those poems (I sometimes recite them in my head when I am on a walk), which explains why I can remember most of them years later.

Or course, I've also forgotten many things I'd once memorized. In college I took two economics courses that required mostly memorization. We copied the notes our teacher put on the board—our exams were based on those notes. Though I aced both courses, I don't remember a single thing I learned in either one. If I'd become an economist, I'd likely have remembered a lot more.

Matching games are not only fun but can help us build our memory skills.
VVOE/SHUTTERSTOCK.COM

Isn't That What's-His-Name?

Many of us have trouble remembering the names of people we've just met. Okay, I'll admit I've sometimes forgotten the name of a student I've taught all semester. Remembering people's names is a useful skill. It's helpful at parties, in the classroom and in business. Calling someone the wrong name can hurt their feelings and possibly lose a sale. Jim Kwik, a brain coach and founder of Kwik Learning and SuperheroYou, is a memory-improvement expert. Here are some of his hacks for helping remember people's names.

- **Realize it's important.** Just telling yourself that remembering someone's name matters increases your chances of being able to remember that name.

- **Focus on the person.** When you are introduced to someone new, focus on that person.

- **Repeat, repeat!** When you first hear the new name, repeat it. "Monique? Isn't that a French name?"

- **Don't be distracted.** No daydreaming allowed!

- **Focus on one of the person's physical features.** Curly hair that could be mistaken for a mop? Check. Remembering one distinguishing physical feature will make it easier to remember that person's name.

- **Create an association.** Monique has hair that could be mistaken for a mop. Coming up with the invented word *Mopnique* may help you remember my name. (The part about the hair is true.)

What Happens When Actors Forget Their Lines?

In the acting industry, forgetting your lines is called *drying*. Even famous actors sometimes dry.

Legendary American stage and screen actor John Barrymore was also legendary for forgetting his lines. Barrymore's memory problems were rumored to have been caused by excessive drinking. Barrymore relied on cue cards.

When Tom Cruise was making the 1990 film *Days of Thunder*, he cheated by taping a sheet of paper to the dashboard of the car he was driving during one of the scenes. Unfortunately, that strategy led to a crash. Fortunately, no one was hurt.

You can't blame the crew of *Saturday Night Live* for forgetting their lines. That's because the show's dialogue is written the day the show is taped. Luckily there's Wally Feresten, aka the Cue Card Guy, whose job it is—you guessed it!—to hold up the cast's cue cards. Bet you wish Wally could be there for your next social studies quiz!

ALL PART OF A DAY'S WORK

For some people, memorizing is part of their job description. Actors, for example, need to memorize a script before the curtains open or the cameras roll. In the next chapter you'll read about actor Marilu Henner, who has a condition called **highly superior autobiographical memory (HSAM)**, which makes memorizing a snap. But how do other actors do it?

Like the rest of us, actors rely on repetition to memorize their lines. In an article for *Backstage* magazine, actor Amy Russ shares her memorization tricks. Whether you're dreaming of becoming a professional actor or you have to memorize your speech for a class presentation, Russ's tricks may prove useful.

- Read your lines out loud. But, Russ adds, it's about more than simple repetition—it's also about thinking. "Knowing what a scene is truly about will help your brain remember lines more easily because there's a story connected to the words," Russ writes.

- Write down your lines.

- Use index cards. Russ advises writing one line per index card, then using the index cards like flash cards. Keep practicing until you can manage without the cards.

- Try a technique Russ calls "first letters." Russ writes down only the first letter of each word she needs to memorize, along with the correct punctuation. With practice, her brain fills in the rest.

- Practice your lines with someone else.

- Use your brain. "Think of your brain like a muscle: the more you practice, the easier it gets," Russ writes.

MEMORIZING HAS AN UPSIDE

Overall, however, memorization gets a bad rap. As a longtime teacher, I took pride in the fact that I seldom asked my students to memorize anything. I always felt a little superior because my focus was on teaching my students to think **analytically** and critically. But it turns out that getting students to memorize material can actually help them when it comes to thinking critically.

According to an article in *Forbes* magazine called "Why Memorizing Stuff Can Be Good for You," expert chess players are not necessarily better analytical thinkers than their weaker opponents. "Rather, they can draw on their vast knowledge of typical chess positions—which they acquired through memorization."

So the next time you have to memorize the names of the world's 10 highest mountains, quit complaining and just do it!

MEMORY SUPERHEROES

8

If you like Marvel Comics, you may know Taskmaster (Tasky for short). This masked assassin only has to watch someone fight once before he can instantly replicate their moves. Which is why Tasky fights as well as Captain America and Spider-Man. In the comic books, Tasky has a *photographic memory*—the ability to recall visual information by taking a quick mental snapshot that can be reviewed later.

SAY "CHEESE!"

Though you may have heard of photographic memory (and long for it when you have to memorize many terms for a test), neuroscientists are not convinced it exists. They prefer the term *eidetic memory*, the ability to naturally and vividly recall things heard, seen or read after only a brief exposure. Unlike photographic memory, which is believed to be based only on what people see, eidetic memory can also involve details gleaned from the other four senses.

Eidetic memory is more common in kids than in grown-ups. It has been estimated that between 2 and 10 percent of children aged 6 to 12 possess eidetic memory. Among neurotypical adults (meaning adults whose neurological function is considered typical), eidetic memory is extremely uncommon. However, an estimated 10 percent of neuro-divergent adults (those whose brains develop or work in nontypical ways) possess eidetic memory.

MEET SOME MEMORY SUPERHEROES

Famous examples include Kim Peek, who could finish a book in an hour and recall the contents of 12,000 books! The 1988 movie *Rain Man*, starring Dustin Hoffman, was based on Peek's story. Peek, an American who was born in 1951 and died in 2009, was considered a **savant** because of his exceptional memory. Peek's father reported that his son began memorizing material at 16 months old. Peek was born with brain abnormalities including **macrocephaly**, meaning his head was larger than average, and something called **agenesis of the corpus callosum**, in which there is a complete or partial absence of the band of white matter connecting the brain's two hemispheres. Some researchers suggest there may have been a link between the absence of Peek's corpus callosum and his increased memory capacity.

Then there is Stephen Wiltshire, a British architectural artist diagnosed with autism at age three. Wiltshire is known for his cityscapes, which he draws entirely from memory. After a 20-minute helicopter ride over New York City, Wiltshire produced a 16.4-foot-long (5.5-meter-long) aerial scene so accurate that even the number of windows in the buildings he drew was correct!

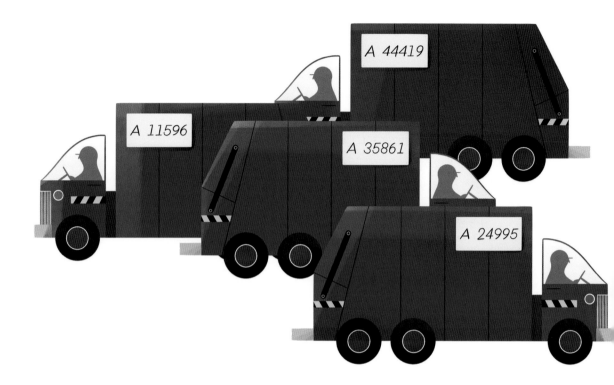

TOTAL RECALL

Although there are some neuroscientists who do not believe photographic memory or even eidetic memory exist, they concede that there are people who have unusually powerful memories and are capable of what seems like total recall. As mentioned in Chapter 7, this condition is called *highly superior autobiographical memory (HSAM)*.

HSAM was identified in 2006 by University of California, Irvine neurologist James McGaugh. His research was based on his work with a woman named Jill Price. If someone told Price a particular date, she could remember what day of the week it was and how she'd spent that day.

Since 2006 more than 50 people have been identified with HSAM, including actress Marilu Henner, author of *Total Memory Makeover: Uncover Your Past, Take Charge of Your Future*, whom you have already read about. When Henner is onstage or in front of a movie camera, she doesn't need a helper holding up cue cards!

Teenager Tyler Hickenbottom is featured in "The Memory Mirage," an episode of CBC's *The Nature of Things*. Hickenbottom loves garbage trucks—he can remember the identification number of every one he has ever seen, records them on video and posts them on YouTube.

No one knows for sure what causes HSAM, but MRI brain scans of individuals with the condition reveal that parts of their brains associated with autobiographical memory appear to be larger than average.

Though having HSAM might sound cool to us, people with the condition complain that it can be a problem. Price uses the word *burden* to describe what it is like to have HSAM. She has also described her memory as "nonstop, uncontrollable and totally exhausting." That's because there is no on-off switch for HSAM.

> *"When we participate actively in our lives and open our senses to all the stimuli around us, we build memories that can be retrieved and enjoyed the rest of our lives."*
>
> —Marilu Henner (1952–), American actress and author

Testing for HSAM

It is estimated that only 60 people on the planet have HSAM. How do you know if you're one of them? Scientists have developed a test with two parts to identify people they call HSAMers. They give the person several dates (for example, December 26, 2004) and ask the person to recall the major news event that happened on each of those dates (on December 26, 2004, the tsunami in the Indian Ocean took the lives of more than 200,000 people). In part two of the test, the person is given 10 random dates and asked to name the day of the week, an event that took place on the day (and which can be verified by researchers) and what the weather was like. The test is scored out of 10. People with normal memory usually get 2 out of 10. The average score for people with HSAM is 9. Markie Pasternak realized she might be an HSAMer as a student at Marquette University in 2014. She was taking a psychology class called Learning and Memory. When the professor explained that some people could remember every day of their lives, Pasternak thought, That's me—I can do that. Pasternak scored a 9 out of 10 on the two-part test.

RELIVING GOOD MEMORIES AND HAUNTED BY BAD ONES

9

Memories—both good and bad—sometimes catch us by surprise. French novelist Marcel Proust is believed to have invented the term ***involuntary memory***. By that Proust meant a memory that seems to pop up out of nowhere but is sometimes triggered by a smell or taste.

In Proust's famous novel *À la recherche du temps perdu* (in English, it's called *In Search of Lost Time* or *Remembrance of Things Past*), the narrator's mother brings him tea and a tiny cake called a madeleine. The narrator dips the cake into his tea, and when he sips it, he experiences what Proust describes as an "all-powerful joy." That's because the smell and taste cause the narrator to remember his childhood days in Combray (a village Proust invented). The narrator finds himself flooded by memories of the aunt who served him tea and madeleines, the old gray house where he lived and the country roads surrounding Combray.

LOOKING BACK AND MOVING FORWARD

The word *nostalgia* is used to describe the complex emotions that arise when we recall happy memories. Feeling nostalgic mostly brings us happiness, but that happiness is sometimes tinged with feelings of sadness or loss. When I smell my grandfather's cigars, I remember the good times we shared, but I also feel the ache of missing him. For more than two centuries, nostalgia was considered a mental disorder characterized by sadness, anxiety and insomnia. The condition was first named in the 17th century by Swiss doctor Johannes Hofer. Hofer based his observations on Swiss mercenary soldiers who had left Switzerland to fight for other countries. He recommended treating these soldiers with leeches or opium or by sending them home. At first nostalgia was believed to affect only the Swiss!

About Those Madeleines

No one has done more to increase the popularity of the little French cakes called *madeleines* than Marcel Proust. In his novel *À la recherche du temps perdu,* the taste of the tea into which the narrator has dipped a madeleine brings him back to his childhood. But it turns out those madeleines could easily have been croissants or chocolate éclairs! French publisher Éditions des Saints Pères revealed that in an earlier draft of Proust's novel, there weren't madeleines at all—there was toasted bread with honey.

For seniors, old photographs can trigger nostalgic feelings and serve as a way to remember their youth.

ELLENAZ/GETTY IMAGES

Today nostalgia is considered normal—and even healthy. In 2012, researchers at England's University of Southampton found that **nostalgic engagement** (a fancy way of saying "remembering happy moments") can be good for us. Their research showed that feeling nostalgic leads to a greater sense of belonging, relieves loneliness, improves our self-esteem and helps us connect with our past selves. These researchers even found that people experiencing nostalgic engagement feel physically warmer than others. Next time you're caught in the cold without a sweater, try remembering a happy moment from your past!

For many of us, nostalgic memories involve being surrounded by loved ones. That may be why Proust's narrator remembered his aunt. It's also common to feel nostalgic about holidays, especially those shared with family and friends.

Spending time with family during holidays can create lasting happy memories. These girls are making paper lanterns called *kandeels* in preparation for Diwali, the Hindu festival of lights.

MEMORIES WE'D RATHER FORGET CAN ALSO BE HELPFUL

Unhappy memories can also catch us by surprise. Researchers have found we are more likely to remember unhappy memories than happy ones. Laura Carstensen, a psychology professor at Stanford University, believes this tendency is rooted in evolution—remembering negative experiences helps us survive. "It's more important for people, for survival, to notice the lion in the brush than it is to notice the beautiful flower that's growing on the other side of the way," Carstensen told the *Washington Post*.

During our lives most of us will experience stressful or **traumatic events**. Trauma can be caused by natural events, such as a flood, or, say, the COVID-19 pandemic. There is also community trauma, such as that experienced by Black North Americans during the time of slavery. Individual

Remembering Trauma

Someone—a person you are getting to know—got my mother to remember the traumatic events of her childhood when she was imprisoned in Theresienstadt, a Nazi concentration camp. If you guessed the person was me, you are correct. In 2007 I decided to write a historical novel for young people based on my mother's childhood experience at Theresienstadt. I spent months interviewing my mother. Though it was difficult for my mother to return in her memory to those dark days, I think she would say the remembering ultimately did her good. For most of her adult life, my mother suffered from insomnia. After sharing the secret she had kept for so long, my mother's insomnia disappeared. And there was no one prouder of the book I ended up writing than my mother!

trauma refers to personal experiences, such as being bullied, attacked or involved in an accident. Memories of traumatic events can be triggered or set off by sensory experiences. For survivors of war, these triggers can include loud banging noises that may remind them of bombs.

When I was growing up, I did not understand why my mother panicked if she spotted a lineup outside the bank. I have already explained that my mother spent nearly two years in a Nazi concentration camp. There she and her fellow prisoners had to queue up in long lines every day for their daily meal—a bowl of watery soup.

Even if Carstensen is right, and remembering trauma has helped humans survive, it is also natural to want to forget or block out bad memories. That was what my mother tried to do. For more than 60 years she refused to discuss what had happened to her during the Holocaust. "I prefer not to remember," she told us.

My mom, Celein Spier, and I are pictured in front of Amsterdam's Hollandsche Schouwburg, where she and other Jews were rounded up by the Nazis in 1943.
MONIQUE POLAK

NEW APPROACH TO BAD MEMORIES

There is some debate about whether revisiting bad memories is helpful or harmful. Some experts warn that asking people to remember difficult experiences can retraumatize them. Alain Brunet, a clinical psychologist and professor of psychiatry at McGill University, studies treatments for **post-traumatic stress disorder** (**PTSD**). Brunet has found a method to help people with PTSD experience their difficult memories in a less painful way. His approach is called **reconsolidation therapy (RT).** One hour before a therapy session, patients are administered propranolol, a blood-pressure and migraine medication that slows the heartbeat and controls anxiety. During the therapy session, patients write a detailed account of their traumatic experience and read it out loud to the therapist. Brunet found that 70 percent of his patients found relief from their PTSD within only a few sessions of RT. Brunet's goal is not to erase traumatic memory, but to make it less painful.

Therapists often listen to their patients recall difficult memories.

10

LET'S GET THIS RIGHT! WHY MEMORIES ARE INACCURATE

I have a crystal-clear memory of meeting Patricia, the girl who lived across the street from us when we were kids. My dad was shoveling snow and I was keeping him company when we spotted her. He put down his shovel and brought me over to meet her.

DON'T BE SO SURE YOU'RE REMEMBERING RIGHT

Fast-forward some 55 years. When I recently shared that memory with Patricia, she said I had it all wrong—that *her* father introduced us! Whose memory is accurate? Mine or Patricia's? We'll never know. That's because our memories of the past are inaccurate.

Researchers have shown that every time we remember a memory, we alter it. We save the alterations in the same way we save changes in a document on our computer. On a computer, we can save every draft and return to the original. However, our memories do not work that way. That's because with every "update," the previous version is lost.

Wayne Sossin, a neuroscience professor at McGill University, studies how memories are retained. He agrees that computers are far better than humans when it comes to storing memories. "The human brain doesn't work as well as a hard drive. We think of human memories as a solid thing, when really they are more fluid," said Sossin. Brenda Milner, the neuroscientist you met earlier in this book, also warned us not to trust our memories. So though my memory of meeting Patricia may feel crystal clear, it's likely wrong!

Because all memories are subject to distortion, they can never be perfect records of the past.
WESTEND61/GETTY IMAGES

IF YOU BUILD IT

It was Milner's professor, Frederic Bartlett, who first recognized that memory is constructive—which means we construct, or build, a memory every time we remember it. The term **Rashomon effect** refers to the fact that different individuals may have differing memories of the same event. *Rashomon* is the name of a 1950 Japanese film written and directed by Akira Kurosawa. It was based on Ryunosuke Akutagawa's short story "In a Grove." In the film (and short story), four witnesses have entirely different memories of a murder. The Rashomon effect doesn't happen only in movies and stories. It has been observed in courtrooms too. Legal cases tend to rely, when possible, on eyewitness testimony. But what if two eyewitnesses remember things differently—and both insist they are right?

CAN MEMORIES LIE?

One of the most debated topics related to memory is whether there is such a thing as **false memory syndrome (FMS)**. The term was introduced in 1992 by Peter J. Freyd, a University of Pennsylvania math professor. Freyd founded the False Memory Syndrome Foundation. The organization folded at the end of 2019, likely in response to the #MeToo movement, a worldwide social movement in support of survivors of sexual harassment and abuse.

The work of American cognitive psychologist Elizabeth Loftus gave some credence to FMS. Loftus asked her students at the University of Washington to devise experiments having to do with memory implantation. One student, Jim Coan, devised an experiment he called "lost in the mall." Coan's first test subject was his 14-year-old brother, Chris. Coan put together four short narratives, purportedly about Chris's childhood. He asked Chris to read and remember them. One of the stories—about Chris getting lost at a mall and being rescued by an elderly gentleman—was untrue. Yet after reading and repeating it, Chris created a new memory about his fictional rescue that he believed to be true. Coan's study, which was later replicated with others, proved that at least in some cases, our memories can be influenced by others.

Getting lost and being separated from their caretakers is a memory kids may carry with them throughout their lives.
MR.YANUKIT/SHUTTERSTOCK.COM

WESTEND61/GETTY IMAGES

Bad Feelings

Negative emotions may interfere with our ability to remember. Brandy Bessette-Symons, an associate professor of psychology at Ithaca College, did a multiyear experiment in which she showed students a variety of pictures that evoked negative emotion, positive emotion or no emotion at all. Ten minutes later and a week later, students were shown the original pictures along with new pictures they had not seen previously. Bessette-Symons found that at both intervals, participants were more likely to falsely identify new pictures that evoked negative emotion, saying these pictures were among the ones they had seen originally. "Emotion doesn't necessarily make us better at remembering. It sometimes makes us worse," said Bessette-Symons.

MOSTLY IN THE MOVIES

But a completely new false memory—such as the one Chris Coan experienced—happens only in a laboratory as part of a scientific study or in the movies! According to Wayne Sossin, a typical false memory is more like my memory of meeting Patricia (or Patricia's memory of meeting me—whichever one of us got it wrong!). "When we make false memories, we usually mix up memories, put two things together and add details that didn't happen so the memory fits in with our view of ourselves and the world," said Sossin.

DARLEINE HEITMAN/SHUTTERSTOCK.COM

Cell Phones Beat Eyewitness Testimony

Cell-phone technology is helping counteract the Rashomon effect. In 2021, police officer Derek Chauvin was sentenced to 22.5 years in prison for the 2020 murder of George Floyd, a Black man suspected of having used a counterfeit bill. Passersby, including then 17-year-old Darnella Frazier, used their cell phones to record Floyd's arrest, during which Chauvin knelt on Floyd's neck and back for more than nine minutes. Frazier's video went viral, sparking worldwide protests against racism and police brutality. When the case went to court, Frazier's video provided irrefutable evidence that Chauvin had murdered Floyd.

ALZHEIMER'S— WHEN FORGETTING ISN'T NORMAL

11

Did you forget to phone your aunt on her birthday? Don't feel too bad. Forgetting is normal.

WHAT'S THAT WORD AGAIN?

Though you've probably never heard the word *lethologica*, it's a kind of forgetting that happens to all of us. Lethologica is when we know a word but cannot think of it. It might be the name of a movie star...or that ice cream flavor you like—you know...the Italian one with layers of different colors and flavors? Spumoni! That's it—spumoni!

> *"I like it when people remember that I'm a person, not just a person with Alzheimer's."*
>
> —Sally Hepworth
> (1980–), Australian writer,
> in *The Things We Keep*

57

Lethologica is a common phenomenon affecting people of all ages. We have the memory, but we just can't access it when we want to. Sometimes the best thing to do is stop trying to remember the word you've forgotten. Then, wham! It may come to you out of nowhere!

FORGETTING SERVES A PURPOSE

Forgetting isn't only normal—it can be helpful. If your heart breaks when your crush just wants to be friends, it's best not to spend the rest of your life remembering that heartbreak. Some neuroscientists believe our brains are built not only to remember but also to forget. If you are bitten by a dog, what you need to remember is that dogs can bite and it's best not to pet one you don't know, not whether tulips were blooming that day. A certain amount of forgetting can help us move forward as individuals and as a species.

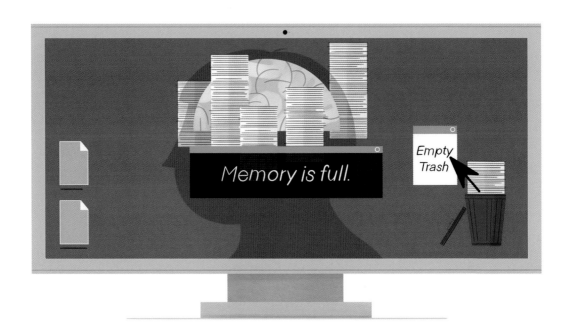

WHERE DID I PUT MY KEYS?

There are many reasons for memory loss. Certain medications, too much alcohol or drugs and lack of sleep can all cause temporary memory loss. Head injuries such as concussions, untreated thyroid problems and strokes can sometimes lead to permanent memory loss.

As we grow older, our ability to remember declines. Forty percent of people over the age of 65 report some memory loss. Most of them are affected by what is called *age-associated memory impairment*. Their memory loss is mild and will not interfere with their ability to look after themselves. They may, however, forget such things as what they were looking for when they walked into the kitchen. If tests show that someone's memory is worse than it was or worse than it should be for someone of their age, the person is considered to have *mild cognitive impairment (MCI)*. For some people, MCI is a normal part of aging. For others, MCI may be an early sign of Alzheimer's disease.

Something as simple as forgetting where you placed your keys can be a natural part of getting older.
PHOTOSCHMIDT/GETTY IMAGES

Taking part in events such as this walk to end Alzheimer's honors those affected by the disease and can help raise money for research into treatments and possibly a cure.

WHEN MEMORY LOSS GETS SERIOUS

Dementia is caused when the brain is damaged by a series of strokes or by certain diseases. In addition to causing memory loss, dementia can lead to mood changes and difficulties with thinking and communicating. Individuals with dementia have functional impairment, meaning they have trouble doing what they did before, such as surfing the internet. Alzheimer's disease is the most common cause of dementia in people over the age of 65.

According to the United Nations, at least 50 million people live with Alzheimer's or some other form of dementia. One-third of people in their 80s have some form of dementia, mostly Alzheimer's. When it affects people younger than 60, the disease is called early-onset Alzheimer's.

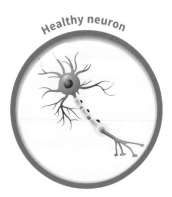

Healthy neuron

The disease is named for Alois Alzheimer, the German doctor who, in 1906, noticed unusual tissue in the brain of a patient who had died with dementia. When Alzheimer examined the patient's brain he found abnormal clumps of protein and collections of broken-down, tangled fibers inside the brain cells. These clumps are now known as *amyloid plaques*, and the snarled fibers are called *tangles*. The presence of amyloid plaques and tangles is a feature of Alzheimer's. Scientists have also observed neuron loss in the brains of people who have died from it.

Behavioral changes are often an early sign of Alzheimer's. It may be difficult for people with Alzheimer's to keep track of time and have conversations. Worsening memory loss leaves Alzheimer's patients unable to take care of themselves.

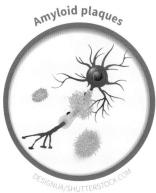

Amyloid plaques

DESIGNUA/SHUTTERSTOCK.COM

CECILIE_ARCURS/GETTY IMAGES

Music to Their Ears

Musical memory is preserved during the early stages of Alzheimer's. A person living with Alzheimer's may remain able to recognize music from their past. It is not uncommon for those who played music to continue to be able to do so even though they have Alzheimer's. If you know someone with Alzheimer's, consider making them a personalized playlist. If possible, try to involve them when you are creating it. Try asking, "What is your favorite kind of music?" You can also research what songs were popular in the years when the person was between 10 and 30 years old. That's because researchers have identified what they call a **reminiscence bump**—the tendency for older people to have more vivid recollections of events experienced during this period.

TESTING FOR MCI

Neurologist Howard Chertkow, director of Toronto's Kimel Family Centre for Brain Health and Wellness, is an international authority on Alzheimer's. Chertkow began studying the disease in the 1980s. "I was interested in memory and language—and why, for example, a person with Alzheimer's might look at a bear and call it a dog," Chertkow explained.

In 2005 Chertkow was part of a team that developed a test called the Montreal Cognitive Assessment, or MoCA. The MoCA is now used worldwide to quickly determine if an individual has MCI. The test assesses areas such as recall of words as well as orientation—which means knowing such things as the date and one's location.

The memory loss associated with Alzheimer's occurs because the tangles are deposited mostly around the hippocampus—you may remember that's the seahorse-shaped part of the brain where new memories are processed. This explains why people with Alzheimer's are unable to recall recent events or conversations. Their old memories, however, tend to be preserved.

PIXELCATCHERS/GETTY IMAGES

Memory Assistance Pooches

Most of us have seen guide dogs assisting individuals who are visually impaired. But did you know there are memory assistance dogs? Israeli social worker Dafna Golan-Shemesh and her partner, dog trainer Yariv Ben-Yosef, developed a program to train dogs to help Alzheimer's patients in the early stages of the disease. Rather than being harnessed like guide dogs, memory assistance dogs are trained to walk ahead of their person on a long leash. Because Golan-Shemesh has worked with people with Alzheimer's, she knows they sometimes become disoriented and have difficulty finding their way home. Memory assistance dogs are trained to respond to the command "home." If they hear that command, the dogs will lead their person to safety. The dogs also provide companionship and an opportunity to go for walks and get some exercise. Both social interaction and exercise can be helpful for individuals living with Alzheimer's.

LOSING MEMORIES

Chertkow describes what it is like to live with mild or moderate Alzheimer's disease: "A person wakes up in the morning, and they're not sure what year it is. They may be 70, but their strongest memories may be from when they were 20. They may be wondering why they are not in the house they lived in at that age, or where their parents are. They feel confused."

Chertkow has a tough job. "It's very sad to see people who lose so much after a lifetime spent building their minds and families. Then they lose their memories," he said. Some of Chertkow's saddest cases involve patients who have survived the Holocaust and now return in their minds to those years they spent in Nazi concentration camps.

As the disease progresses, most individuals with Alzheimer's become unaware of what they have lost. "The disease often becomes more and more difficult for families. Alzheimer's disease changes behavior and personality. Some individuals become angry and aggressive, even with their loved ones," said Chertkow. One of his patients forgot where she had put her gloves and accused relatives of stealing them.

Alzheimer's is also devastating for the friends and family of the person who has it, some of whom may become caregivers. Many friends and family members report feeling grief and anger after a loved one's diagnosis. Looking after a person with Alzheimer's can be overwhelming. When patients require round-the-clock care, their families may opt or may have to move them to long-term facilities.

STILL THE SAME PERSON

Chertkow has this advice for young people who have a grandparent with the illness: "Even if the person doesn't remember who you are, or behaves in ways you are not accustomed to, it's important to remember it's still the same person."

For now there are no drugs to prevent the disease. There are drugs, however, to treat patients during the early and mid stages of Alzheimer's. Chertkow hopes there will someday be drugs to prevent Alzheimer's in at-risk individuals and prevent MCI from progressing to Alzheimer's dementia. Much research is being done to identify risk factors associated with developing Alzheimer's. "There are genetic elements, but there are many lifestyle factors we can control to help prevent Alzheimer's," Chertkow said.

Spending time with children has been shown to improve the mood and stimulate the brains of individuals with Alzheimer's.

IRYNA KHABLIUK / EYEEM/GETTY IMAGES

WAYS TO PREVENT ALZHEIMER'S DISEASE

- **Get educated**. Every year of schooling reduces the risk of developing Alzheimer's.

- **Learn more languages**. Speaking three or more languages reduces the risk of developing Alzheimer's.

- **Don't bang your head**. Preventing head injuries in sports reduces the risk of developing Alzheimer's. "From an Alzheimer's point of view, nobody should play football," said Chertkow.

- **Go for regular checkups**. Untreated high blood pressure, diabetes and obesity all increase the risk of developing Alzheimer's.

- **Eat green, leafy vegetables and avoid too much meat**. Following what is known as the Mediterranean diet can reduce the risk of developing Alzheimer's.

- **Get your zzz's**. Seven to eight hours of sleep every night helps the brain clear out amyloids.

- **Breathe clean air**. Exposure to air pollution increases the risk of developing Alzheimer's.

- **Make friends**. Depression and loneliness increase the risk of developing Alzheimer's.

- **Protect your ears**. Hearing loss increases the risk of developing Alzheimer's. Avoid loud concerts. Get your hearing tested. Middle-aged people who need hearing aids should get them.

- **Floss daily**. Certain oral bacteria increase the risk of developing Alzheimer's.

12

HISTORY AND COLLECTIVE MEMORY

"History is written by victors." Most people attribute this famous quote to Winston Churchill, former prime minister of the United Kingdom. But Churchill may not have said it first. Some scholars attribute the quote to Napoleon Bonaparte or Mark Twain. Which shows how difficult it can be to get the past right.

SHARED MEMORIES

History is the study of past events. As we have already seen, our personal memories—even if they are sometimes inaccurate—help tell the stories of our lives. The term *collective memory* refers to how groups remember a shared past. Though countries cannot form memories, their inhabitants can and do. Groups of people who have undergone similar experiences share collective memory. The same is true for smaller groups such as your family or your kindergarten class.

According to psychology researcher Henry L. Roediger III, "to understand a country's memories is to grasp something essential about their national identity and outlook." In an article that Roediger cowrote with K. Andrew DeSoto, he gives the example of how different countries remember World War II. Americans tend to remember the attack on Pearl Harbor that brought the United States into the war. But when Russians remember World War II, they tend to focus on another event—the Battle of Stalingrad, during which two million of their soldiers were killed or captured. Roediger and DeSoto also explain that collective memories can change over time.

Poppies pinned to lapels sometimes fall off. That may be why people are coming up with new ways to use poppies for Remembrance Day.

RMC42/SHUTTERSTOCK.COM

A Day for Remembering

Every year on November 11, citizens of Commonwealth countries, including Canada, the UK and Australia, honor the memory of soldiers who have died in the line of duty. Remembrance Day was introduced by King George V on November 11, 1919, to mark the one-year anniversary of the end of World War I. Canadians pause at 11 a.m. on November 11, taking a moment of silence to remember those who gave their lives for their country. It was 11 a.m. on November 11, 1918, when fighting officially ended. Many Canadians also mark the day by wearing a felt poppy on their coats. The fields in Flanders, Belgium, where some of the worst battles of World War I occurred, were chalky and barren before the war. The many bombs created rubble, causing the chalky soil to become rich in lime—ideal growing conditions for poppies. These red poppies grew over the graves of the soldiers who had perished during the war.

REMINDERS TO REMEMBER

A *memorial* is an object created to remind us of a person or event. In a way, a memorial is a call to remember. Here in Montreal, one of the first things you see when you walk into Westmount High School is a bronze tablet commemorating the young men from the school who served in the Canadian Army during World War I. On the two side panels are the names of 384 of these young men. On the center panel are the names of the 58 others who never returned from overseas. To this day the memorial is a sobering reminder of the sacrifices previous generations made for their country.

WINNING DESIGN

One of the world's most famous memorials can be found on the National Mall in Washington, DC. The Vietnam Veterans Memorial is a giant V-shaped black-granite wall with the names of the nearly 58,000 American servicemen and women confirmed dead or missing in action during the Vietnam War. It was designed by American architect and sculptor Maya Lin. At the time, Lin, the daughter of Chinese immigrants, was an architectural student at Yale University. Lin's professor encouraged her to enter her design in the competition for the memorial. It was one of more than 1,400 submissions. Lin was in her dorm in May 1981 when she learned her design had been chosen for the memorial. Quite an accomplishment for a 21-year-old!

At first Lin's memorial was controversial. Vietnam War veteran Tom Cathcart was upset that the memorial was black, which he described as "the color of shame and sorrow and degradation." Others objected because they felt the V-shaped design was anti-war—that the V resembled the two-finger peace sign used by anti-war protesters.

Eventually the controversy subsided, and the memorial has become an important place to come for those who served in the war—and the people who loved them.

The Vietnam Veterans Memorial in Washington, DC, attracts more than five million visitors a year.
ROLF_52/SHUTTERSTOCK.COM

Remembering the Holocaust during the COVID-19 Pandemic

During the COVID-19 pandemic, museums and public spaces around the world had to close their doors. Organizations whose goal it is to help us remember major historical events scrambled to devise new ways to commemorate.

The Montreal Holocaust Museum's most important commemorative event of the year is Yom HaShoah—Holocaust Remembrance Day. Before the pandemic, the event was always held at a local synagogue, with about 1,400 people attending. Sarah Fogg, the museum's head of communications, was part of the team that came up with a new way to mark the occasion online.

"We got people—Holocaust survivors, people from the museum and the community—to record from their homes."

More than 6,000 people watched the museum's first online Yom HaShoah commemoration in April 2020. "It was very special to be together, especially on such a solemn, holy day. It allowed us to build a community outside Montreal. People from around the world heard the survivors' stories," said Fogg.

The pandemic proved that people are open to new ways of commemorating.

Transmitting the memory of the Holocaust is one of the museum's chief missions. "There is also the human rights legacy," said Fogg, "and the lessons we have to remember: to speak up when you see injustice, to fight against hate—anti-Semitism, racism or other forms of discrimination—and to be respectful and tolerant of diversity."

RECENT CONTROVERSIES ABOUT LONG-STANDING MEMORIALS

In recent years some memorials that have been around for a long time have become the subjects of controversy. In Montreal more than 10,000 people signed a petition asking the city to remove a bronze monument in the heart of downtown. The monument is a statue of Sir John A. Macdonald. Canada's first prime minister, Macdonald established the country's **residential school system**, which removed some 150,000 Indigenous children from their families. In addition to being taken away from their families and communities, and losing much of their culture and language, many of these children were abused, and more than 6,000 children died in the residential school system. In the words of the Honorable Murray Sinclair, who served as chair of the Truth and Reconciliation Commission of Canada: "What took place in residential schools amounts to nothing short of cultural genocide—a systematic and concerted attempt to extinguish the spirit of Aboriginal peoples."

On Halloween of 2019, protestors covered the statue with spray paint. The next summer the statue was pulled down.

Protesters challenge the legendary status of the first US president, George Washington, who owned hundreds of enslaved people during his lifetime.
SHIVA PHOTO/SHUTTERSTOCK.COM

A City of Montreal advisory committee recommended the statue should not be put back. In its preliminary report, the committee wrote, "In the spirit of the reconciliation process, it is necessary to distance ourselves from this legacy of John A. Macdonald."

Many Torontonians wanted to see the statue of Egerton Ryerson removed from the campus of the university that had been named in his honor. In his role as chief superintendent of schools for Ontario between 1844 and 1876, Ryerson recommended that Indigenous children be sent to residential schools. His statue was vandalized many times. In June 2021 the statue was toppled, and the university decided to remove it from the campus. In 2022 the university's name was changed to Toronto Metropolitan University.

These examples prove that collective memory can change as we reach a deeper and more sensitive understanding of the past. Perhaps history need not be written only by white males. When we bring our modern-day sensibilities, knowledge and perspective, we help reshape and refine collective memory.

In 2021 these children's shoes were displayed on Ottawa's Parliament Hill after the discovery of burial sites at former residential schools.

GARY A CORCORAN ARTS/SHUTTERSTOCK.COM

BEARING WITNESS TO THE PAST

The world's approach to memorials is also being reshaped and refined. A powerful example is the Witness Blanket, a traveling art installation that will be on permanent display at the Canadian Museum for Human Rights in Winnipeg. The Witness Blanket brings together material objects that help tell the story of Canada's residential schools. Created by carver, sculptor and storyteller Carey Newman, the Witness Blanket consists of almost 900 objects, many of which came from the schools, ranging from photos and letters to skates and even braids of hair. As Newman explained, "A common method of extinguishing cultural identity was to cut the children's hair when they first arrived at school." Newman's own father, a Survivor of the residential school system, still remembers what a traumatic experience this was.

In gathering these objects, Newman was asking Survivors of the residential school system, including his father, to remember a terrible time in their lives—a time some might have preferred to forget. Newman has this to say about the process: "Darkness keeps things hidden away...Even though it might feel easier or safer to keep traumatic memories locked away, eventually they need to come out into the light."

This is a portion of the Witness Blanket, which includes photographs and reclaimed objects from former residential schools across Canada.
MEDIA ONE INC.

MEMORY—A SOURCE OF INSPIRATION

13

I've waited till the last chapter of this book to tell you why I'm so interested in memory. It's because as a reader, writer and longtime writing teacher, I've observed how memories are a huge source of creative inspiration. And it's also because I am fascinated by research showing that how we remember our pasts is a creative act, and that in remembering, we are in a way creating ourselves. So I wanted to learn more about how memory works.

"The future doesn't exist. The only thing that exists is now and our memory of what happened in the past.

But because we invented the idea of a future, we're the only animal that realized

we can affect the future by what we do today."

—David Suzuki (1936–),
Canadian environmental activist

MAKE ROOM FOR MEMORY IN YOUR TOOLBOX

Creativity means using imagination together with skill to solve a problem or produce something new, such as an invention or work of art. According to Art Markman, a psychology professor at the University of Texas at Austin, "Creativity is driven by memory." As Markman writes in *Psychology Today*, "Whenever you are in a situation in which you need to solve a creative problem, you need to find ways to reach into your memory to find information that will be relevant to solving the problem."

Here's an example. Say you live in Montreal, where it gets awfully cold during winter, and when you put your key into the door lock, your key breaks in two! That's a problem that needs solving—and doing so requires creativity.

Perhaps you remember that several winters ago your best friend's key also broke on a winter day, and his mom used a neighbor's hair dryer to warm up the keyhole and free the piece of key stuck in the lock. So you borrow a hair dryer to deal with the problem. Memory helped you find a creative solution to your problem.

DMYTRO TYSHCHENKO/SHUTTERSTOCK.COM

INVENTOR'S IDEAS GROW LIKE MUSHROOMS

Inventor Eben Bayer's most famous invention was inspired by a childhood memory. Bayer, who lives in New York, is a mechanical engineer who invented a biodegradable packaging material to replace Styrofoam. Raised on a farm in Vermont, as a child Bayer sometimes helped his father shovel wood chips. Bayer remembered looking down from the top of the wood-chip pile and noticing what looked like spiderwebs. But they were mycelium—the vegetative part of a fungus. Bayer also remembered that mycelium are naturally gluey. So he found a way to make packaging material from mycelium.

Eben Bayer and his team are currently working on ways to use mushroom mycelium to make gourmet foods.

MYCOBOND/WIKIMEDIA COMMONS/ CC BY-SA 2.0

Unlike Styrofoam, Bayer's invention—now used around the world—is good for the environment. Tossed into the water after use, it makes excellent fish food. On land it's perfect for the compost pile.

GETTING PERSONAL ON THE PAGE

Sometimes memory inspires works of art. Perhaps you have heard the word **memoir**. A memoir is a personal account of someone's life—or perhaps a period of that person's life. Writing a memoir begins with remembering. Just as we have seen how memories are reshaped with every telling, the memoir writer reshapes the past by selecting which parts to tell, which parts to omit and, of course, which words to use.

Becoming is an example of a well-known memoir. Written by Michelle Obama and published in 2018, *Becoming* is a deeply personal account about Obama's youth, struggles she faced to become a lawyer and her relationship with her husband, former US president Barack Obama. The memoir provides an inside peek into the White House and reveals Michelle Obama's devotion to her family. When the Obamas moved to the White House, Michelle's mother moved in with them.

COURTESY BARACK OBAMA PRESIDENTIAL LIBRARY

In 2020 Michelle Obama's memoir, *Becoming*, was made into a documentary film released on Netflix.

FAIZAL RAMLI/SHUTTERSTOCK.COM

STIRRING UP CONTROVERSY

James Frey's *A Million Little Pieces* is one of the most controversial memoirs of our time. Published in 2003, the book was marketed as a memoir about Frey's drug addiction and how he overcame it. Only after the book had become a bestseller did allegations surface that some of the material in the book had been invented. For example, Frey had described being jailed—but when reporters investigated, they learned this had never happened. Frey was held at a police station for several hours but never put behind bars.

In 2006 Frey was dropped by his literary agent. Readers who felt they had been tricked were offered a refund of the book's purchase price. Frey appeared on the *Larry King Show* and *Oprah*—making him and his book even more famous. Frey has argued that all memoirs alter details: "Some people think memoirs should be held to a perfect journalistic standard. Some people don't. Obviously I don't. My goal was never to create or to write a perfect journalistic standard of my life." In 2009 Oprah Winfrey called Frey to apologize for having shamed him on her TV show.

EMOZAK/SHUTTERSTOCK.COM

I'M A WRITER, YOU'RE A WRITER!

Even if we never put words on paper or write our memoirs, we all "write" the story of our lives. This happens when we remember our pasts and tell others—or even just ourselves—what we have lived through. We all find material in our memories and demonstrate creativity when we reframe our experiences in the form of a reminiscence told aloud, in a journal or in a published book. Here's a question for you to think about now and as you grow up: Are you the hero of your own life? Is your story a hopeful one?

Researchers are studying the connection between how we remember our pasts and how we see ourselves and feel in the present. They see all of this behavior as creative. "You are your story," writes Christian Jarrett in an article for the BBC. Jarrett explains that "how you interpret your life, and tell its story, has profound effects on what kind of person you become."

If to be a writer is to use written words to communicate ideas, then we can all be writers.

MILLANN/GETTY IMAGES

Mining Memory Exercise

When I do writing workshops for kids, I share my theory about memory. "Memories," I tell the students, "are stories asking to be told." Here's an exercise I use to help young writers mine their memories and come up with something interesting to write about. A special shout-out to Canadian editor Peter Carver, who first introduced me to this exercise.

The exercise works best when your eyes are closed, so you might ask someone else to read you the instructions.

Remember back to when you were five years old. If your mind lands on an incident, that's great. If your mind is jumping around, that's also fine. See if your mind lands on one scene. What do you see? Are you inside or outside? What season is it? Do you see other people?

What do you hear? Is there a dog barking? Are kids singing "Happy Birthday"? Do you hear whispers from another room?

If you could go back into the memory, what would you be able to touch? Your grandmother's hand squeezing yours? Your cat's tail as he brushes against you?

What do you taste? Is there a taste associated with your memory of being five?

What do you smell? Suntan lotion? Spaghetti sauce? The garbage truck passing on a sweltering day?

Now, with your eyes closed, put together everything you remembered—what you saw, heard, touched, tasted and smelled. Open your eyes and jot down everything that came to mind. Your answer can come out in note form or in sentences or a paragraph. Could what you remembered become the basis for a story? Consider asking yourself the question "What if?" Change up the memory to add drama to your story.

GOOD CAN COME OUT OF BAD

Narrative therapy helps people examine the storyline they have constructed for their lives and adjust that storyline to feel better about their lives. Researchers have found that individuals who look back at a difficult period of their lives and are able to identify what positive effects came out of it tend to be happier than those who dwell on the negatives. Someone who was bullied in the schoolyard in second grade may look back at that experience and realize it taught them compassion and resilience, and to stand up for those who need help.

There is even a phrase to describe narrative strategies or storytelling styles that can help us reframe our memories in a more positive way: ***redemptive sequences***. We make use of redemptive sequences when we consider how a bad or emotionally negative experience led to something positive.

Remembering these difficult experiences can force us to grow in unexpected ways.
MOMO PRODUCTIONS/GETTY IMAGES

Goes Both Ways—Creativity Can Improve Memory

As we have seen, memory can inspire creativity. But certain kinds of creativity—such as playing a musical instrument—can actually improve memory. According to Anita Collins, author of *The Music Advantage: How Music Helps Your Child Develop*, *Learn* and *Thrive*, musicians have "enhanced memory functions." That, Collins explains, is because musicians are accustomed to giving memories many tags, so their brains store a memory in several places—which improves their ability to remember. In a TedEd talk on how playing an instrument benefits the brain, Collins explains that musicians are capable of "creating, storing and retrieving memories more quickly and efficiently. Studies have found that musicians appear to use their highly connected brains to give each memory multiple tags, such as a conceptual tag, an emotional tag, an audio tag…like a good internet search engine."

Muzna Dureid works as a liaison officer for the White Helmets, a volunteer organization providing aid in Syria and Türkiye.

DAVID BOILY/LA PRESSE

COURAGE TO QUESTION

Muzna Dureid was 20 when she fled Syria in 2011. Dureid had been and remains an activist, standing up against the regime of Bashar al-Assad. Dureid's worst memory is of nearly being detained when she was going through customs at the Damascus airport. When the customs officer seemed to know Dureid's phone number, she had to act quickly. "It meant the government was monitoring me. I knew they would arrest me. So I said it wasn't my number. Then I took out my phone and put it on airplane mode. And I gave him another number," Dureid recalled. The officer made Dureid wait a half hour before telling her she could go. Dureid went straight to the washroom, where she put on glasses and a scarf in hopes she would not be recognized if the customs officer realized who she was. She did not cry—not until she was safe in the sky. "When we were over the clouds and I could no longer see Syria, I finally cried—out of relief, and also because I knew it was the last time I'd see my country," said Dureid.

More than a decade later, Dureid continues to recall that harrowing ordeal. But with time she has come to see what she gained from the experience. "It was worth it. As a woman, I gained control over my life, body and beliefs. I also learned to question everything around me. No issue is taboo. It gave me the courage to question," Dureid told me.

Dureid's reframing of that difficult memory is an example of a redemptive sequence.

THE GIFT OF MEMORY

We can all learn from our pasts. Hopefully, nations can learn too and avoid making the same mistakes over and over again. Without the gift of memory, this learning and the ability to make change would not be possible.

While researching this book, I learned that memory is a far more complicated and less reliable phenomenon than I'd thought. But I also learned that memory is a precious gift. Memory helps us connect with others—and ourselves. May you use your gift of memory in ways that are creative, that help you grow and that help make the world a better place for all of us!

GLOSSARY

age-associated memory impairment—mild memory impairment in people aged 65 and older that does not interfere with their ability to look after themselves

agenesis of the corpus callosum—a condition in which there is a complete or partial absence of the band of white matter connecting the brain's two hemispheres

Alzheimer's disease—a degenerative brain disease that causes the brain to shrink and brain cells to die, leading to the deterioration of memory and thinking skills

amnesia—memory loss, usually temporary, due to such things as brain injury, shock and illness

amygdala—the part of the brain associated with emotion

analytically—using logical reasoning

attention-deficit/hyperactivity disorder (ADHD)—a brain disorder which causes such problems as difficulty paying attention, sitting still or controlling behavior

cerebral cortex—the outermost layer of the brain, associated with processes including memory, language, thought, decision-making and emotion

collective memory—how groups remember a shared past

constructive—in terms of memory, a type of recollection in which we build on or add detail to a memory every time we remember it

dementia—an impaired ability to remember, think or make decisions, caused when the brain is damaged by strokes or by certain diseases, such as Alzheimer's, which is the most common cause of dementia in people over the age of 65

eidetic memory—the ability to naturally and vividly recall things heard, seen or read after only brief exposure

encoding—the first step in creating a memory, which happens when we learn something or when information comes to us through the five senses

episodic memory—autobiographical memory of a specific past event or episode

executive functions—brain functions that help us plan ahead and achieve our goals

false memory syndrome (FMS)—a controversial theory stating that false memories can be implanted; also the experience of seeming to remember events that never occurred

flashbulb memory—a memory associated with learning about a major, usually disturbing, public event

highly superior autobiographical memory (HSAM)—a rare condition in which people have unusually powerful memories and are capable of what seems like total recall

hippocampus—the region located deep in the brain where new memories are processed and sent off to other parts of the brain

involuntary memory—a memory that seems to pop up out of nowhere but is sometimes triggered by a smell or taste

lethologica—inability to recall a word even when we know it and it's on the tip of our tongues, a common phenomenon that affects people of all ages

limbic system—the part of the brain involved in emotional and behavioral responses

long-term memory—memory involving information that is stored and recalled over a long period of time. Long-term memories are stored in many parts of the brain—there are five distinct areas in the brain that store memories for each of the five senses.

macrocephaly—a brain abnormality in which the head is larger than average

memoir—nonfiction personal writing about an individual's life or a period of it

memorial—an object created to remind us of a person or event

memory triggers—any stimuli that cause us to recall memories

mild cognitive impairment (MCI)—a condition in which people have more thinking and memory problems than other adults of the same age. Individuals with MCI may have some difficulty speaking and are at higher risk of developing Alzheimer's disease.

mnemonics—techniques used to improve memory

muscle memory—the ability to repeat a particular movement without having to think about it, acquired through repetition

narrative therapy—a psychotherapeutic approach that helps people examine the storyline they have constructed for their lives

nostalgia—the complex emotions that arise when we recall happy past times

nostalgic engagement—remembering happy moments from our pasts, which can have a beneficial effect

olfactory bulb—part of the brain that runs from the nose to the base or front of the brain and receives neural input about odors

photographic memory—the ability to remember visual information by taking a quick mental snapshot that can be recalled later (neuroscientists are not sure that this ability really exists)

post-traumatic stress disorder (PTSD)—a psychological reaction that can occur after experiencing a traumatic event or series of events

prefrontal cortex—a region of the brain that has many functions, including storage of short-term memories

procedural memory—long-term memory of how to do such things as playing piano

Rashomon effect—the idea that individuals may have differing memories of the same event (the term comes from the Japanese film *Rashomon*)

reconsolidation therapy (RT)—a therapeutic approach to help individuals with PTSD experience their traumatic memories in a new, less painful way

redemptive sequences—memories reframed to focus on how a bad or emotionally negative experience led to something demonstrably positive

relevance—the state of being personally meaningful, a factor that may influence the development of a flashbulb memory

reminiscence bump—the tendency for elderly people to have vivid recollections of events they experienced between the ages of 10 and 30

residential school system—a system implemented by the Canadian government that forcibly separated Indigenous children from their families and forbade them to speak their languages or acknowledge their cultures. It began in the 19th century and continued well into the 20th century.

retrieval–calling up information from memory when we need it

savant—a person who is exceptionally skilled in a particular field or with abilities such as an unusually powerful memory

semantic memory—long-term memory for general accumulated information that is not connected to particular events or contexts

short-term memory—memory that involves information we need to recall for a short amount of time, stored in the brain's prefrontal cortex

souvenir—an object that serves as a memento to help us remember a place, experience or person, or sometimes all three

storing—how we hold on to memories over time

thalamus—the part of the brain whose job it is to relay information to the cerebral cortex

transitional objects—objects that have significance because they were with us when we moved from one stage of life to another, such as blankets and teddy bears, which can help us get through difficult periods

traumatic events—incidents that cause physical, emotional and/or psychological harm. They can be natural events or experiences such as being abused, bullied or attacked.

working memory—the system that allows us to store and work with information for a relatively short time

RESOURCES

PRINT

De Goldi, Kate. *The ACB with Honora Lee.* Tundra, 2017.

Dellis, Nelson. *Memory Superpowers! An Adventurous Guide to Remembering What You Don't Want to Forget.* Abrams Books for Young Readers, 2020.

Gill, Leanne Boucher. *Big Brain Book: How It Works and All Its Quirks.* Magination Press, 2021.

Gill, Leanne Boucher. *Lobe Your Brain: What Matters About Your Grey Matter.* Magination Press, 2021.

Karosen, Kent, and Chana Stiefel. *Why Can't Grandma Remember My Name?* Fisher Center for Alzheimer's Research Foundation, 2016.

Marshall, Lisa. *Memory Improvement for Kids: The Greatest Collection of Proven Techniques for Expanding Your Child's Mind and Boosting Their Brain Power.* Montessori Parenting, 2020.

Stoddard, Lindsey. *Just Like Jackie.* HarperCollins, 2018.

Teckentrup, Britta. *The Memory Tree.* Hachette, 2014.

Toner, Jacqueline B., and Claire Freeland. *Psychology for Kids: The Science of the Mind and Behavior.* Magination Press, 2021.

Van Draanen, Wendelin. *The Secret Life of Lincoln Jones.* Yearling, 2016.

ONLINE

Alzheimer's Association: alz.org/help-support/resources/kids-teens

Art of Memory: artofmemory.com

Brain Canada Foundation: braincanada.ca

Brain Facts: brainfacts.org

Creative Writing Now: creative-writing-now.com

Ducksters: ducksters.com/science

Improve Memory: improvememory.org

Memorize Now: memorizenow.com

Memorizer: memorizer.me

Memozor Memory Games: memozor.com

National Geographic Kids: natgeokids.com

National Institute on Aging: nia.nih.gov/health/helping-children-understand-alzheimers-disease

Nemours KidsHealth: kidshealth.org

Neuroscience for Kids: faculty.washington.edu/chudler/introb.html

Understood: understood.org/en/articles/how-memory-works-in-kids

ACKNOWLEDGMENTS

Many thanks to the experts who agreed to be interviewed for this book and who taught me so much: neurologist Howard Chertkow; activist Muzna Dureid; filmmaker Jon Fein; and neuroscientists Rachel Herz, Brenda Milner and Wayne Sossin. Thanks also to Geneviève Alexander and Kyra Simatos, both of whom I had the pleasure of teaching at Marianopolis College and who shared important memories with me. Giant thanks to the terrific team at Orca Books, including editorial assistant Georgia Bradburne, designer Dahlia Yuen and my superb editor, Kirstie Hudson, who believed in this book from the very start. A big thank-you to Valéry Goulet, whose thoughtful and fun illustrations help bring my words to life. A special thanks to my own in-house neuroscientist, my partner, Guy Rouleau.

INDEX

*Page numbers in **bold** indicate an image caption.*

Monique Polak is the author of more than 30 books for young readers and the three-time winner of the Quebec Writers' Federation Janet Savage Blachford Prize for Children's and Young Adult Literature (formerly called the QWF Prize for Children's and Young Adult Literature). Monique is an active freelance journalist whose stories appear across the country. She recently retired after a long and happy career teaching English and humanities at Marianopolis College, and now devotes herself to writing full-time. Monique lives in Montreal.

Valéry Goulet is a French Canadian designer, illustrator and design instructor originally from Quebec. With a master's in interaction design from Université Laval, she's worked with global brands and agencies, and her illustrations have garnered attention far and wide. When she's not illustrating, Valéry instructs for the Visual Communication Design program at the University of Alberta and the Bachelor of Design program at MacEwan University. She lives in Edmonton.